NATURE WATCH

CARNIVOROUS PLANTS

Written by
Rebecca L. Johnson

Lerner Publications Company • Minneapolis

Lerner Publications Company
A division of Lerner Publishing Group
241 First Avenue North
Minneapolis, MN 55401 U.S.A.

Website address: www.lernerbooks.com

Library of Congress Cataloging-in-Publication Data

Johnson, Rebecca L.
Carnivorous plants / by Rebecca L. Johnson.
p. cm. — (Nature watch)
Includes index.
ISBN-13: 978-0-8225-6563-5 (lib. bdg. : alk. paper)
ISBN-10: 0-8225-6563-3 (lib. bdg. : alk. paper)
1. Carnivorous plants—Juvenile literature. I. Title.
QK917.J64 2007
583'.75—dc22 2006018982

Manufactured in the United States of America
1 2 3 4 5 6 - DP - 12 11 10 09 08 07

Contents

A green tree frog sits on a colorful white-topped pitcher plant in Alabama.

Amazing Carnivorous Plants

The plant looks so inviting. Its delicate leaves are covered with tiny hairs. Each hair is topped with a glistening drop.

A hungry fly lands on one of the leaves. But it quickly discovers that the shiny drops aren't food. They're incredibly sticky goo. The fly struggles to pull free. But it only touches more of the sticky drops. Suddenly, the leaf begins to move. It curls slowly down and around the struggling insect *(shown above)*. It hugs the fly in a deadly embrace. In fact, it has already started to eat the fly, its latest catch.

A plant that catches and eats animals? It may sound like science fiction. But it's not. Welcome to the world of carnivorous plants.

A damselfly is caught on a sundew plant.

Green Meat Eaters

The plant is a sundew. It's just one of many kinds of carnivorous plants in the world. The word *carnivorous* comes from two Latin words, *carne* and *vore. Carne* means "meat." *Vore* means "to eat." So something that's carnivorous is a meat eater.

When most people think of meat eaters, they think of animals such as lions or sharks. They don't usually think of plants. We've heard a lot about animals that catch and eat other animals. The idea of plants that catch animals is a little unsettling. But that's just one of the things that makes carnivorous plants so interesting.

Because they catch animals, carnivorous plants are **predators.** A predator is a living thing that catches and eats animals for food. The animals that a predator eats are called its **prey.** The sundew's prey are flies and other small insects.

To be considered carnivorous, a plant must do several things. It must attract, or lure in, its prey. Then the plant must somehow catch the prey and kill it. Finally, the plant must digest what it has caught. *Digest* means to "break down food and **absorb** its **nutrients.**"

Most of the animals that carnivorous plants eat are crawling and flying insects. They might eat flies, gnats, or moths. Also on the menu for some carnivorous plants are spiders, pill bugs, worms, and frogs. A few large carnivorous plants have been known to eat birds, mice, or rats. But this is very rare.

An opened Venus flytrap reveals the remains of a digested spider.

FOOD AND NUTRIENTS

Despite their unusual appetites, carnivorous plants are still plants. Like other plants, they carry out **photosynthesis.** This process allows plants to make their own food out of water and carbon dioxide. Carbon dioxide is a gas in the air. You breathe out carbon dioxide every time you exhale. Using energy from sunlight, plants turn water and carbon dioxide into sugar and oxygen. Oxygen is another gas in the air. Your cells need oxygen to live. You breathe in oxygen every time you inhale.

Plants also take up water, minerals, and nutrients through their roots. Carnivorous plants do this too, just like all their regular plant cousins.

But if carnivorous plants can do what other plants do, why do they catch and eat animals? The answer has to do with their **habitats.** Habitats are the types of places where carnivorous plants live and grow. Carnivorous plants tend to live in habitats where the soil is poor. Poor soil contains few minerals and very little **nitrogen.** Nitrogen is a nutrient. Living things use it to make proteins, the building blocks of cells. More often than not, soils poor in nutrients and minerals are also wet. So if you want to find carnivorous plants, some of the best places to look are swamps, bogs, and rain forests.

Carnivorous pitcher plants, like all plants, carry out photosynthesis to make most of their own food.

During photosynthesis, plants release oxygen into the air. In fact, plants make much of the oxygen that people breathe in. In this way, plants help people to survive. Plants also help other animals to survive. From mice to elephants, all animals need to take in oxygen with every breath.

Just as plants help animals to survive, animals can be helpful to plants. Plants make food from the carbon dioxide that animals exhale.

Purple pitcher plants grow in a bog in Chequamegon-Nicolet National Forest in northern Wisconsin.

In these places, carnivorous plants don't just survive. They thrive. That's because carnivorous plants don't rely only on nutrients in soil or those made by photosynthesis. They also take nutrients from the animals that creep, crawl, and fly all around them. Carnivorous plants may live in nutrient-poor habitats. But they are surrounded by food in the form of their prey.

Although carnivorous plants are surrounded by food, they have to catch the food before they can eat it. Fortunately, the plants meet that challenge very well. Over time, they have developed many tricks and traps to snare flies, ants, beetles, and other creatures. The meals they catch are a rich source of the nutrients that are missing from the soils in which they grow.

A World of Hungry Plants

Carnivorous plants grow on every continent except Antarctica. About 15 major groups of carnivorous plants exist. Scientists call each of these groups a **genus** (JEE–nuhss). (The plural of genus is genera.) Each genus contains several different types, or species, of plants. The world has at least six hundred species of carnivorous plants.

Every carnivorous plant has one or more common names. But each has only one scientific name. That name includes both the genus and species names. For instance, the pink sundew *(shown above)* grows in parts of North America, Central America, and South America. It has different common names in all these places. But it has only one scientific name: *Drosera capillaris.*

MANY SHAPES AND SIZES

Carnivorous plants come in many sizes. The largest are tropical pitcher plants. These plants belong to the genus *Nepenthes.* They grow in damp, humid jungles in Southeast Asia, Indonesia, Madagascar, and northeastern Australia. The traps of these carnivorous plants are shaped like big vases or pitchers. The traps of *Nepenthes rajah,* a native of Borneo, are the largest of all. They grow up to 14 inches (35 cm) long by 7 inches (18 cm) wide!

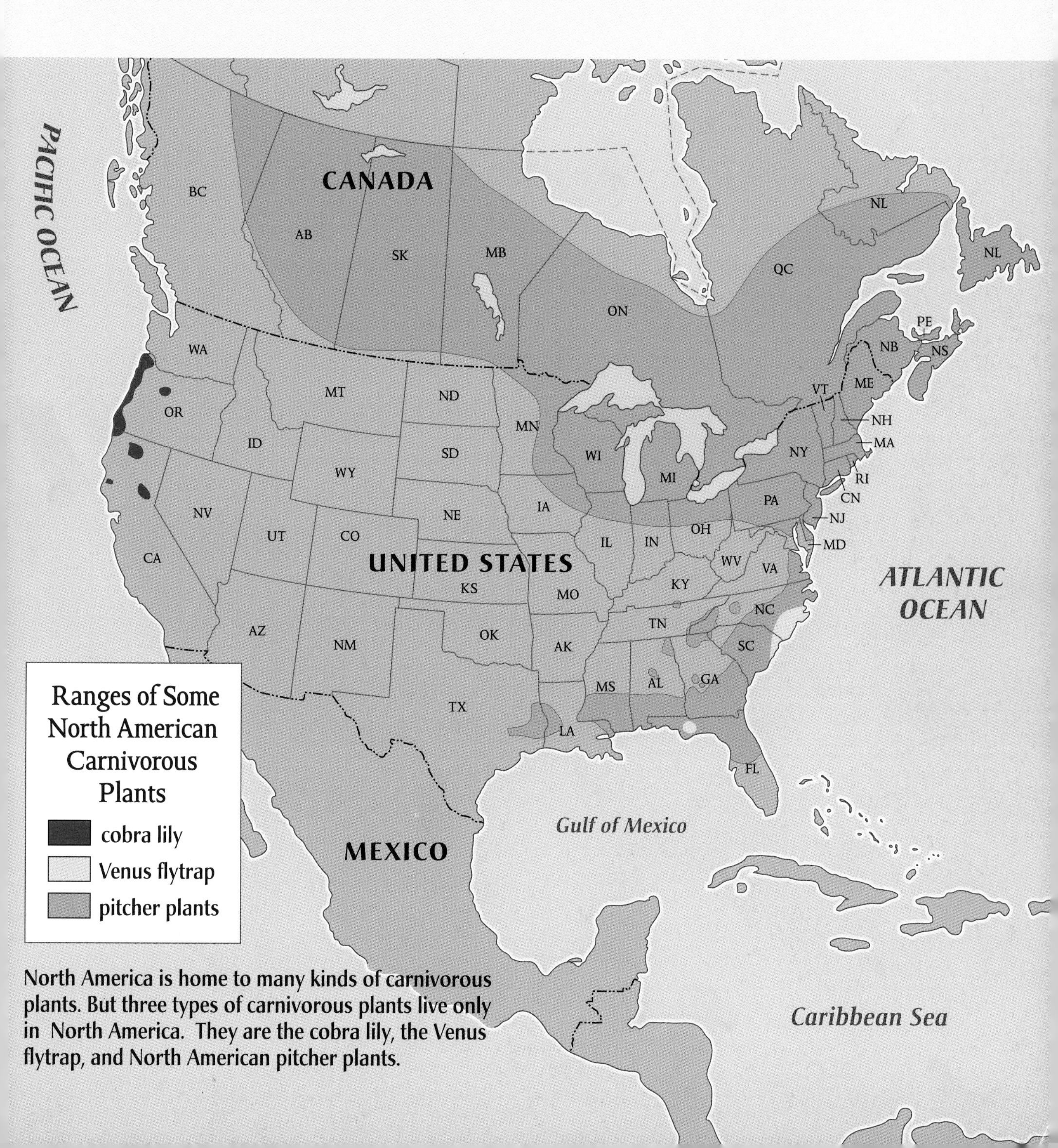

North America is home to many kinds of carnivorous plants. But three types of carnivorous plants live only in North America. They are the cobra lily, the Venus flytrap, and North American pitcher plants.

This close-up view of colorful pygmy sundew plants shows the rosettes, or circular bunches of leaves, on the plant.

Pygmy sundews live mainly in Australia. They are among the world's smallest carnivorous plants. Most pygmy sundews are no larger than a penny. And most grow low to the ground. Many pygmy sundews have spoon-shaped leaves. The leaf tips are rounded and scooped out in the middle. The leaves grow in tight circles called rosettes.

Carnivorous Plant Variety

Many other carnivorous plants fall somewhere in between these two size extremes. The variety seems almost endless. Some are tall. Others hug the ground. Some have long, delicate parts. Others have stout and rounded bodies. Still others grow as vines, twining their way through shadowy forests.

Carnivorous plants may be brightly colored, vivid green, or somewhat drab. Some have huge flowers. Others have tiny blooms that are easy to miss. But no matter what their shape or size or color, all carnivorous plants are deadly. They'll make a meal out of any creature unlucky enough to fall or fly into their traps.

Most tropical pitcher plants are good climbers. They grow as thick vines that send out long, twisting tips from some of their leaves. These tips are called tendrils. Tendrils curl around whatever they touch. In this way, they grab onto stems and branches of other plants. With the help of their tendrils, some pitcher plants may climb 50 feet (15 m) above the forest floor.

Carnivorous plants come in all shapes and sizes, including the trumpet pitcher plant *(right)* and cobra lily *(below)*.

When a Leaf Is Not a Leaf

Carnivorous plants have many differences. But they also have one thing in common. They all have some kind of trap for catching insects or other prey. In most carnivorous plants, these traps are formed from **modified** leaves. (*Modified* means "changed to have a different shape or function.") Some plants' traps are more modified than others.

A pitcher plant's trap *(shown above)* is not very modified. It looks a lot like a typical leaf. In fact, imagine taking a large, flat leaf and rolling it into the shape of a funnel. It would look a lot like the trap of a pitcher plant. The trap has a wide, open top that narrows toward the bottom. You can see veins in the trap, just like you can in a regular leaf. In some pitcher plant traps, there is a ridge along one side. The ridge resembles a seam, as if the trap were a regular leaf that had been stitched or glued together.

Nectar isn't the only substance carnivorous plants use to lure prey. Some give off the odor of decay. A plant that smells like rotting meat might seem unpleasant to us. But flies can't resist it.

Shiny surfaces that look wet also help attract prey to traps. So do glistening drops. Both drops and shiny surfaces offer the promise of a cool drink. Many traps have flat parts that form perfect landing pads for insects. Bright colors also work to lure in potential prey. Some carnivorous plants combine these tricks. Their brightly colored traps look wet and give off an irresistible odor.

Carnivorous plants use many tricks to get prey to land on them. The butterwort has leaves that look shiny and are easy for insects to land on.

This ant is trapped on the sticky leaf of a round-leaved sundew. The insect will be digested by the plant, and the insect's nutrients will be absorbed through the leaf.

DIGESTION

Once they've trapped and killed their prey, carnivorous plants must digest it. Most carnivorous plants produce **digestive juice.** Digestive juice breaks down the bodies of insects and other creatures. It turns tissues and cells into a nutrient-rich liquid. Carnivorous plants absorb the nutrients from this liquid through the walls of their traps.

A few kinds of carnivorous plants get help with this digestive work. Some have traps that are full of **bacteria.** Bacteria are one-celled living things. They are so small you'd need a microscope to see them. When prey are caught in the traps of these plants, the bacteria do most of the digesting. They turn the bodies of prey into nutrient soup. The plant then absorbs this ready-made meal.

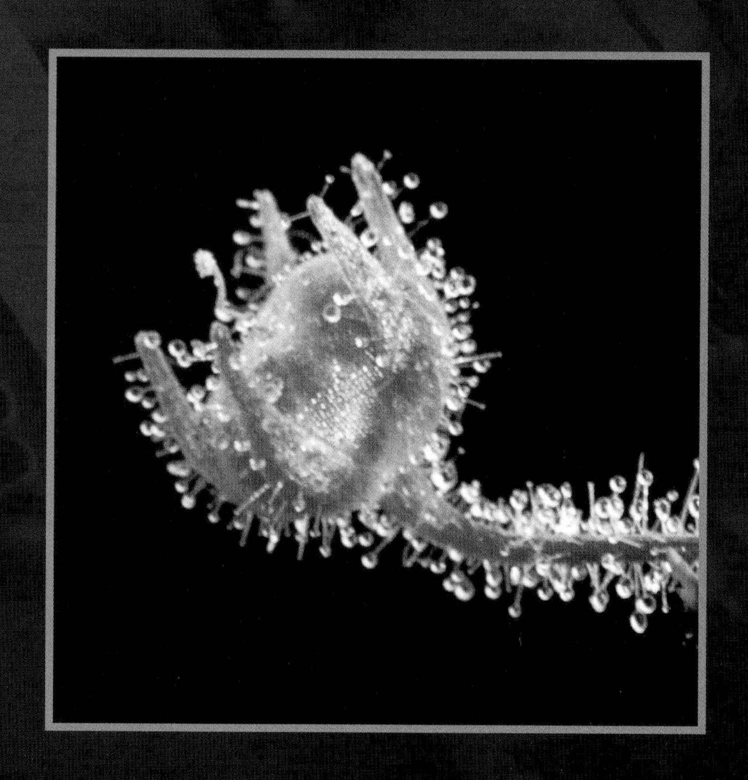

Passive Traps: Sticky Pads and Pitfalls

Carnivorous plants come in many different forms. But **botanists** (scientists who study plants) often group them into two basic types. There are those that have traps with moving parts. And there are those with traps that don't move at all. Traps with moving parts are known as active traps. Traps that do not move are called passive traps.

Carnivorous plants with passive traps wait for prey to get into trouble all by themselves. Passive traps might not seem as exciting as movable, active traps. But they are just as effective at killing prey. The rainbow plant's trap *(shown above)* is a good example.

A gnat is about to be captured by this rainbow plant, *Byblis liniflora*.

Rainbow Plant Traps

Rainbow plants grow only in Australia. They belong to the genus *Byblis.* There are just six species. One of these is *Byblis gigantea.* As carnivorous plants go, this one is fairly big. It grows up to 2 feet (0.6 m) tall. *Byblis liniflora* is a much smaller rainbow plant. It reaches only 9 to 12 inches (22–30 cm) in height.

Rainbow plants have narrow leaves. The leaves are covered by many tiny stalks. A clear drop of liquid caps each of these stalks. The liquid is a lot like glue. The plant's stems are also crowded with drop-topped stalks. As a result, the whole plant seems to shimmer in rainbow colors. It looks as if it's covered with thousands of tiny jewels.

Rainbow plants can be beautiful. But beware their sparkling jewels! Insects and other creatures that touch any part of the plant quickly get stuck. Rows of digestive glands lie among the sticky stalks. They produce digestive juice that digests freshly caught prey. Rainbow plants catch a surprising number of insects and spiders on their leaves and stems. Sometimes they're nearly completely covered by them.

Corkscrew Traps

The corkscrew plant has one of the most complex passive traps in the carnivorous plant world. More than one dozen species of corkscrew plants make up the genus *Genlisea.* They grow in tropical regions of South America, Africa, various Caribbean islands, and Madagascar. Corkscrew plants live in water rather than on land. Their traps sprout by the dozens from long, narrow stems. The traps vary from 1 to 6 inches (2–15 cm) in length.

A single trap is made up of a small bulb-shaped pouch. The pouch has a small tube growing out of it. The end of the tube splits into two branches. Each of these branches twists, or spirals, like a corkscrew.

Water creatures enter the trap at the tip of one of the branches. Around and around they go, following the spiral path. Eventually they reach the tube. But once inside this part of the trap, they find themselves surrounded by rows of

Corkscrew plants live in water. This corkscrew plant's blooming flowers rise above the water's surface.

sharp hairs. The hairs point inward. They make it impossible for the trapped creatures to back up. So they keep moving forward—until they reach the pouch. The pouch is full of digestive juice. The trapped creatures cannot escape. They become the corkscrew plant's next meal.

Pitcher Plant Traps

Pitcher plants make up one of the largest groups of carnivorous plants. Botanists group dozens of known pitcher plant species into several genera. Pitcher plants come in different shapes and sizes. But all of them catch prey in a similar way. They have pitfall traps. A pitfall trap is open at the top and closed at the bottom. Insects and other prey simply fall into it. Once inside, they can't get out.

Pitcher plants' trumpet- or pitcher-shaped traps have a pool of liquid at the bottom. The pool is made up mostly of digestive juice. Insects are attracted to the pitcher by its bright colors or sweet nectar. They land on or crawl up onto the rim. They walk around, eating or exploring. If they wander too close to the edge of the rim, they slip off. They tumble down into the pool at the bottom of the trap. The walls of the pitcher are too slippery to climb. The insects drown in the pool. Then the pitcher plant digests them.

Trumpet pitchers grow mostly in eastern North America. They range from central Canada to the southeastern United States. They thrive in wet meadows and along damp coastal plains.

All trumpet pitchers belong to a single genus: *Sarracenia.* And all have a similar trap. It's a tall, thin trumpet-shaped tube. In many cases, the trumpet has a lidlike hood that arches over the opening at the top.

The outside surface of the pitcher is covered with nectar-producing glands. Most of these glands are near the top of the trumpet. The greatest number line the curved rim surrounding the opening. The glands around the rim ooze sweet nectar. The rim glistens as if wet. To an insect, it looks inviting. But the rim is also very slippery.

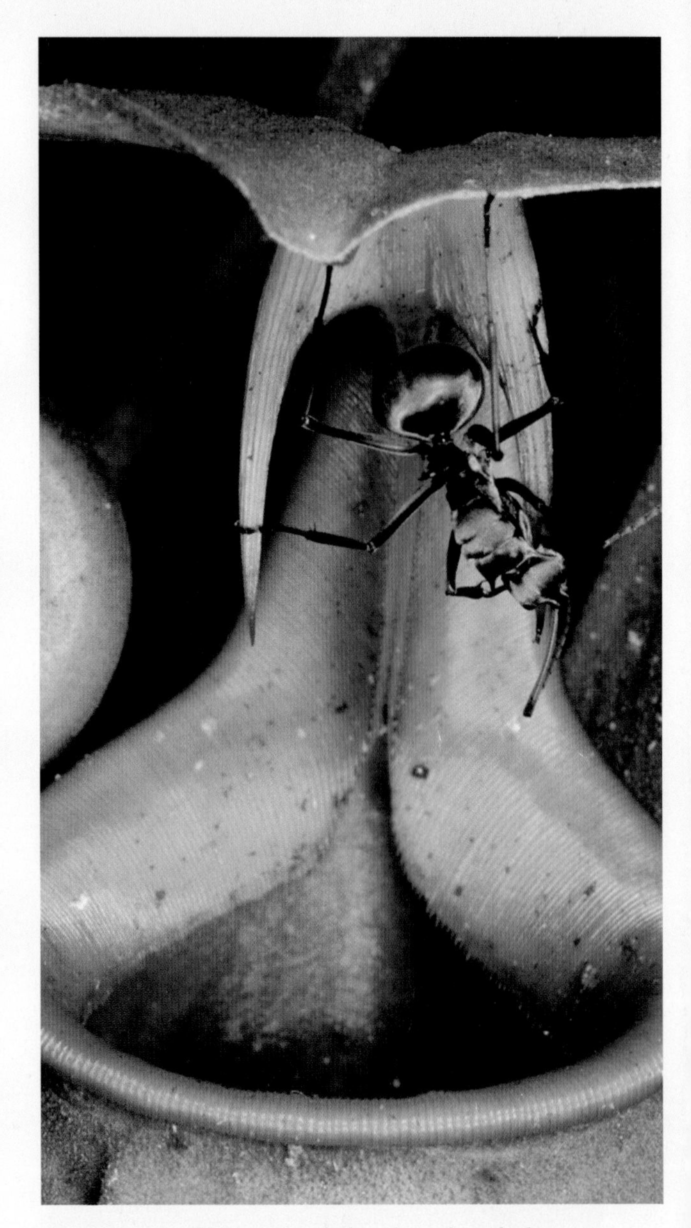

An ant scrambles around the rim of a pitcher plant in Borneo. Nectar glands cover the surface of the slippery rim.

This pitcher plant's trap glistens and appears wet at the top, enticing prey to land on it. Some prey will lose their grip and will slide down into the pitcher to the pool of liquid at the bottom.

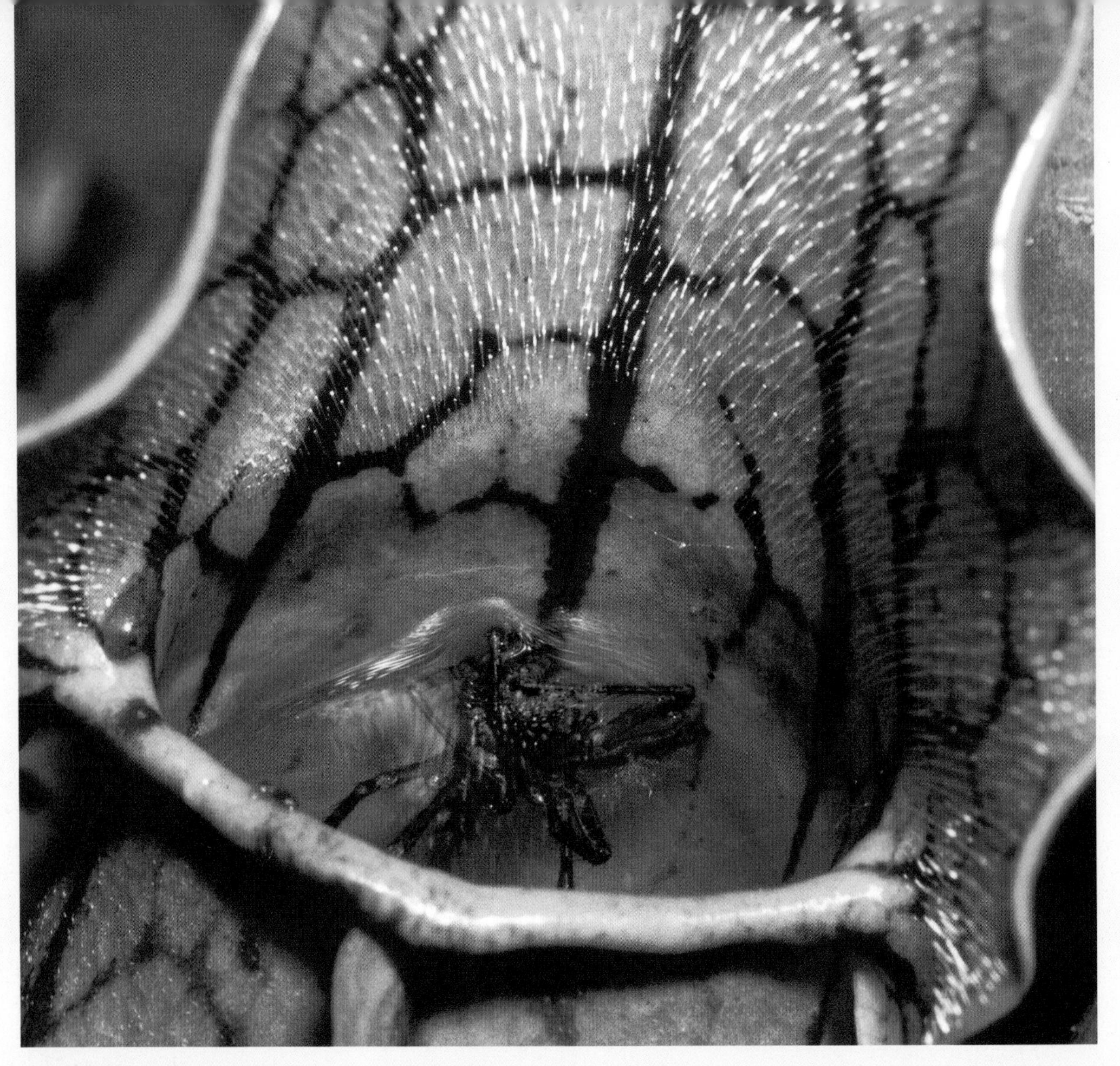

This spider fell into the liquid at the bottom of a pitcher plant.

Nectar glands cover the inside of the trumpet's rim too. Below the rim, the inside walls of the trumpet are coated with wax. They are also dotted with digestive glands. Further down inside the trumpet are long, sharp, down-pointing hairs. At the trumpet's very bottom is its pool of digestive juice.

Some trumpets are quite beautiful. Their traps are edged with red, yellow, and orange. The sweet scent of nectar surrounds them. Ants and other insects arrive to investigate. Following the nectar glands, they make their way to the rim. Many wander close to the rim's inner, slippery edge. If they go too far, they lose their grip. They fall into the trumpet and the liquid at its bottom.

The inner walls are as smooth as glass. The down-pointing hairs help make escape impossible. For a few minutes, trapped insects struggle to climb out of the pool. But soon they grow still and digestion begins.

The cobra lily *(Darlingtonia californica)* is closely related to trumpet pitchers. It grows in cool, wet regions of coastal Oregon and northern California. This plant is named for the cobra, a type of snake. The top of the plant's trap looks a little like a cobra's hood (a flap of skin and muscle that the snake flares when threatened).

The tip of the trap's hood extends as two points. Some people think this tip resembles a snake's forked tongue. This tongue-shaped extension is packed with nectar glands. Insects land on it and crawl into the trap. Inside the trap are clear patches that look like small windows. When insects have had their fill of nectar, they head for the patches. They look like the way out of the trap. But it's a trick. The patches and the rest of the trap's inner surface are very slippery. Insects can't hang on. They slide down the walls of the trap. They end up in the liquid at the bottom.

The cobra lily can be found in cool, wet areas of California and Oregon.

The traps of the West Australian pitcher plant are particularly strange looking. *Cephalotus follicularis,* as scientists call it, grows in only one small region along Australia's southwestern coast. It thrives in swamps and areas of wet sand.

The traps of this carnivorous plant are short and squat. They form a circle on the ground around the plant. The pitchers have three ridges that insects, especially ants, often follow. The ridges lead to a ribbed rim where hundreds of nectar glands glisten. As is the case in other pitcher plants, many insects lose their footing as they feed along the slippery rim. They fall into the pool at the bottom of the pitcher. Then they drown. Finally, the plant digests them.

Many species of tropical pitcher plants make up the genus *Nepenthes.* Tropical pitcher plants are climbing vines. They wind themselves around trees and bushes. They hang on with ropelike tendrils that grow out from the tips of long, flat leaves. Pitcher-shaped traps form at the tips of some of these tendrils. Traps range from just a couple inches in size to more than 1 foot (0.3 m) long and wide.

When a trap is fully formed, its lid pops open. Down at the bottom is a pool of digestive juice. Insects land on the rim of the pitcher to feast on nectar. Many tumble to their death in the liquid inside. The plant digests gnats and mosquitoes within hours. It might take two days to digest a large fly or spider. The pitchers of tropical pitcher plants are often heavy with trapped and digested insects. It's not unusual to find scorpions, centipedes, and even larger prey.

The West Australian pitcher plant has a ridged rim around the pitcher. Insects often lose their footing when they land on the rim, and they fall into the pool at the bottom of the pitcher.

Tropical pitcher plants come in many different shapes, sizes, and colors.

Active Traps: Tricky Traps That Move

SOME OF THE MOST AMAZING CARNIVOROUS PLANTS HAVE traps with parts that move. These active traps allow the plants to capture even fast-moving prey. They also bring prey into contact with digestive glands very quickly. The faster digestion takes place, the faster a meal's nutrients are absorbed.

Butterwort Traps

Different kinds of active traps move at different speeds. The leaves of butterworts *(shown above)* move slowly. Butterworts (genus *Pinguicula*) grow as flat rosettes of yellow green leaves. The leaves are pretty. They shine. If you touch them, they feel greasy. It's as if the leaves were coated with butter. The coating is produced by special glands on the leaves. Along with these glands are thousands of digestive glands.

When a small insect lands on a butterwort leaf, it gets stuck in the grease. As it struggles, the digestive glands pump out digestive juice. While this is happening, the edges of the leaf slowly curl up. The inner part of the leaf may also sink down. This forms a dip under the insect's body. The dip fills with digestive juice. Both movements help **concentrate** digestive juice directly around the trapped insect. The insect eventually drowns in all this digestive juice. Sometimes the juice begins to break down the insect's body even before it's dead.

A fly is trapped on the sticky surface of a butterwort plant.

Sundew Traps

Remember the sundew you met at the beginning of this book? It's a carnivorous plant that acts quickly to catch and kill its prey. Sundews belong to the genus *Drosera.* There are more than one hundred species. Sundews are found in most countries. They often grow in bogs. The exception is Australian sundews, which live in drier habitats.

There is no such thing as a typical sundew. They vary a great deal in size and shape. Some sundews have leaves only a fraction of an inch long. Others have leaves that are 2 feet (0.6 m) in length. Leaves may grow up from the ground or hug the soil in a tight circle. They can be narrow and straplike or shaped like circles or spoons.

The leaves of all sundews, though, are covered with long tentacles. The tentacles are capped with sticky, glistening drops. At first glance, the drops look like dew on the leaves. These dazzling dewdrops attract insects. But

This round-leaved sundew, *Drosera rotundifolia,* has an inchworm trapped on its sticky tentacles.

The long leaves of the *Drosera filiformis,* a kind of sundew plant, roll up around the prey after it gets stuck on the plant's tentacles.

when an insect lands on a leaf, it is instantly stuck. Nearby tentacles begin to move. They bend toward the struggling insect. They curl around it, hugging it tighter and tighter. If the insect was caught near the leaf's edge, the tentacles move it toward the leaf's center. That's where digestive glands are concentrated.

In some sundews, the entire leaf also moves. The long, straplike leaves of *Drosera filiformis,* for instance, roll up around new victims. They curl around them tightly. This concentrates digestive juice around them.

Round-leaved sundews such as *Drosera rotundifolia* have leaves that widen at the tips into spoon shapes. When an insect lands on a leaf, the tentacles grip it first. Then the entire spoon-shaped tip folds around the insect. It's like a hand closing up into a fist.

Pygmy sundews form small, neat rosettes of leaves. In some species, the whole plant is just 0.5 inch (1 cm) across. Like some larger relatives, pygmy sundews have spoon-shaped leaves. They also close around newly captured prey.

Fork-leaved sundews grow in mountain bogs and other soggy habitats in Australia and New Zealand. They are some of the strangest looking of all carnivorous plants. As their name suggests, fork-leaved sundews have long, spindly leaves that divide, or fork, at their tips. Sometimes they fork more than once. This produces plants that look like a cluster of tiny deer antlers. Long tentacles cover each forked leaf. First, the tentacles grip an insect unlucky enough to bump into this sundew's deadly branches. Then the entire leaf curls around it. It's a double grip from which there is no escape.

A fork-leaved sundew's first leaves are not divided. They are small and round, and they have no tentacles. The next leaves are also round. But they're slightly spoon-shaped. They're longer and narrower, and tentacles are present on the leaves. They resemble the leaves of a pygmy sundew. The leaves that follow are longer and narrower still. Eventually, the plant sends up very thin leaves that fork at the tips.

This close-up look at a fork-leaved sundew plant shows how the leaf ends can curl up around prey.

The Venus flytrap has trigger hairs on the inside of its trap. When an insect touches these hairs, the trap snaps shut.

The Venus Flytrap

Perhaps the best-known carnivorous plant is one with very active traps. The plant is the Venus flytrap. Its scientific name is *Dionaea muscipula.* The Venus flytrap was the first plant that people suspected was carnivorous. This isn't really surprising, because when a Venus flytrap is feeding, it really does resemble a savage beast.

The traps of a Venus flytrap form at the tips of specialized leaves. Each trap has two halves called **lobes.** Lobes are rounded, fleshy leaf structures that are hinged together along one edge. The free edges are fringed with 15 to 20 long, sharp spines. The trap looks a bit like the steel traps that people once used to catch wild animals.

When the trap is open, the lobes are spread wide. They make a nice, flat surface. It's a perfect landing pad for a fly. The surface of each lobe is covered with thousands of glands. Some produce nectar. Others produce digestive juice.

Three small hairs project from the middle of each lobe in the trap. As a fly or other insect walks around, lapping up nectar, chances are good it will bump into the hairs. The hairs are like triggers. When an insect touches them in just the right way, the trap snaps shut. It shuts so fast that if you blink, you might miss it.

Inside the trap, the insect becomes a prisoner. It is locked behind the spines. The more the insect struggles, the tighter the lobes squeeze together. Their edges seal. The pressure is so great that the insect is often crushed. Digestive juice oozes from glands on the lobes. The trap turns into a stomach. The fly becomes a meal.

It takes a week or two for a Venus flytrap to digest such a catch. When the nutrients from the meal have been absorbed, the trap opens again. It is ready to snare something else.

These photos show a damselfly landing on a Venus flytrap *(above)*, then getting caught in the trap when it snaps shut (*right*).

These bladderworts are growing in a wetland.

Bladderwort Traps

The traps of Venus flytraps move fast. But those of bladderworts are even faster. Bladderworts are the speed champions in the world of carnivorous plants. More than two hundred species are grouped together in the genus *Utricularia.* Bladderworts are found worldwide. Most live in water. But some make their home in damp sand or soil.

A bladderwort's traps are rounded pouches, or bladders. These are usually not much larger than the head of a pin. But there may be dozens, even hundreds, of bladders on a single plant. At one end of each trap is a tiny trapdoor. It can swing inward but not outward. By a clever mechanism, the bladderwort pumps water out of its bladders. This creates a **vacuum** inside them.

Tiny trigger hairs surround the trapdoor of a bladder. When a small creature, such as a water flea, touches the trigger, the trap is sprung. If you could slow down the action, you'd see that first the trapdoor swings inward. Then the flea is sucked into the bladder as water from outside rushes in. Finally, the trapdoor swings shut. All of this happens very fast. It takes only 10 to 15 thousandths of a second!

The trapped water flea may live for several hours inside its tiny prison cell. But eventually it dies. The bladderwort digests it and absorbs the nutrients.

The bladderwort has dozens of small rounded traps that look like pouches all over its branches.

LIFE CYCLES

CARNIVOROUS PLANTS USE REMARKABLE TRICKS TO CATCH food. Sometimes it's easy to forget that they share many traits of typical plants. Just like their plant cousins, carnivorous plants **reproduce.** Reproduction is a key part in any plant's life cycle.

Nearly all carnivorous plants produce flowers. Their flowers are as different as their traps. Some species produce great clusters of blossoms. Others send up a single flower stalk. Some flowers are big. Others are dainty.

The tiny white flowers held high above a Venus flytrap *(shown above)* seem out of place considering the ready-to-snap traps lurking below! The big flowers of trumpet pitcher plants grow on stalks 1 to 3 feet 0.3–0.9 m)

The flowers of a pitcher plant rise above the rest of the plant.

It's not surprising that many carnivorous plants have flowers that stand high above their traps. The plants need bees to pollinate their flowers. If the flowers were very close to the traps, bees might be caught and killed. Flowers would go unpollinated. Seeds wouldn't form. Plants would not be able to reproduce. Bees are more important to carnivorous plants as pollinators than they are as food.

high. They can be 4 inches (10 cm) across and bloom for several weeks. Butterworts produce white, pink, or purple flowers. They tower on sturdy stalks above greasy leaves.

Pollen and Reproduction

The flowers produce tiny grains of yellow, powdery pollen. Bees and other insects pick up some of these pollen grains. At each flower they visit, bees leave behind some of the pollen stuck to their bodies. Pollen grains that land on the **pistil** of the flower form a tube that grows down to the pistil's base. There, the grains deliver sperm cells to tiny egg cells. Eggs and sperm unite to form seeds. When the seeds are ripe, they break out of the structure that holds them. Seeds that land in suitable spots will **germinate.** Then they'll begin to grow into new plants. This starts the cycle all over again.

A green sundew with a flower atop one of its branches

This is the flower of a giant rainbow plant (*Byblis gigantea*). *Byblis gigantea* can go dormant when conditions around it are dry. Going dormant allows it to survive.

Beyond Seeds

A few types of carnivorous plants reproduce in less common ways. Pygmy sundews produce flowers that form seeds. But the sundews can produce tiny **gemmae** (JEH–mee) as well. Gemmae (also called brood bodies) are miniature copies of the adult plant. They are smaller than the heads of pins. Raindrops help scatter the gemmae. Those that land in suitable spots take root.

As part of their life cycle, some carnivorous plants can also go **dormant** when growing conditions are not good. A dormant plant is not actively growing. The rainbow plant *Byblis gigantea* usually grows on the edges of swamps. During the winter, the swamps are very wet. But in summer, the swamps sometimes dry out. When this happens, the leaves of the rainbow plant die. Safe beneath the soil, belowground parts survive until fall. That's when the rains return. The swamp refills with water. Wet again, *Byblis gigantea* sends up new tentacle-studded leaves. The cycle starts over.

Carnivorous Plants and People

WHETHER THEY START FROM SEEDS, GEMMAE, OR BY SOME other means, young carnivorous plants can grow only in the right habitats. They need water and sunlight. They need the right temperature and enough soil. And, of course, young carnivorous plants need plenty of insects and other small creatures for food.

About 30 years ago, there were many wild, wet habitats throughout the world. Carnivorous plants thrived in these places. But many of those habitats are gone. Countless swamps and bogs have been drained. People have cleared them to build houses, roads, and shopping malls. Offices and condominiums line coastal areas where wetlands once stood *(shown above)*. As more people need more space, habitats for carnivorous plants keep slipping away.

Plants in Danger

Many species of carnivorous plants have become scarce in places where they once were common. In fact, some species are **endangered** in the wild. *Endangered* means "at risk of dying out." Wild-growing Venus flytraps are endangered. If we don't protect and preserve their habitats, some types of carnivorous plants may soon become **extinct.** Living things that are extinct are no longer alive anywhere on Earth.

Preserving Carnivorous Plants

But carnivorous plants are getting some help. Collecting wild carnivorous plants is illegal in most parts of the United States. It's illegal in many other countries too. People caught collecting plants in protected areas must pay large fines. They may even go to jail.

Groups concerned about preserving carnivorous plants are buying land that is home to their habitats. The groups work to keep the land safe and wild. In other places, people are restoring wetlands and other places carnivorous plants live.

Botanists have learned new ways to grow large numbers of some carnivorous plants. Under special conditions, small pieces of plant tissue can be kept alive in test tubes. The pieces grow into entire

These young Venus flytraps are growing inside near a window.

Until recently, people used to collect wild carnivorous plants. They planted them in their gardens. They tried to keep them as houseplants. But carnivorous plants can be hard to grow. They need special conditions, just like those in their natural habitats. Plants taken from the wild often died quickly. Other carnivorous plants were collected to replace them. It didn't take long before very popular species began disappearing in the wild.

Some plant nurseries specialize in carnivorous plants. These nurseries sell seeds and cuttings so people can raise the plants indoors.

plants. This method of raising plants is called tissue culture. Using tissue culture, it's possible to raise thousands of plants in a very short time.

When the greenhouse was invented in the 1800s, a new type of gardening was born. People began growing exotic plants in greenhouses year-round. In the United States, raising carnivorous plants indoors caught on as a hobby in the middle of the 1900s. It has been gaining in popularity ever since.

Many species of carnivorous plants can be started from seeds. Others can be started from small pieces, or cuttings, of adult plants. Plant nurseries that specialize in carnivorous plants sell seeds and cuttings. They also sell adult plants started through tissue culture. Anyone with a little patience and the right materials—you, perhaps?—can grow some types of carnivorous plants. Once you get started, you might want to join the International Carnivorous Plant Society. It's a group with thousands of members in many countries. Members share information about carnivorous plants. They hold meetings around the world. Joining the club is a good way to keep exploring the wonderful world of carnivorous plants.

GLOSSARY

absorb: to take in

bacteria: one-celled living things that cannot be seen without a microscope. Some carnivorous plants digest their food with the help of bacteria.

botanists: scientists who study plants

concentrate: to come together in one place

digestive juice: a fluid that breaks food down into smaller forms that can be absorbed and used by a living thing

dormant: not actively growing; in a resting stage

endangered: at risk of dying out

extinct: no longer living on Earth

gemmae: small, immature forms of a parent plant. Gemmae are also called brood bodies.

genus: a group of plants or living things that share common characteristics. A plant genus contains several different types of plants.

germinate: to sprout and begin to grow

glands: small plant and animal parts that make different kinds of liquid substances, such as nectar or digestive juice

habitats: the types of places where a kind of plant or animal can live and grow

lobes: rounded, fleshy leaf structures that are hinged along one edge

modified: changed to have a different shape or function

nectar: a sweet liquid produced by plants to attract insects or other small animals

nitrogen: a nutrient used by living things to make proteins and other substances needed for life

nutrients: substances needed for life

photosynthesis: the process by which plants use energy from the sun to make their own food (sugar) out of water and carbon dioxide

pistil: the female part of a flower, which houses egg cells at its base

pollen: powdery grains produced by flowers. Flowering plants need pollen to produce seeds.

predators: living things that catch and eat animals for food

prey: the animals caught and eaten by a predator

reproduce: to make new living things of the same kind

species: type of plant or living thing. Plants in the same genus can be further grouped according to what type, or species, they are.

tendrils: long, twisting tips of stems or leaves

tentacles: long, thin, movable structures that can bend and grab

vacuum: a space that is empty of air and at a lower pressure than the surroundings

SELECTED BIBLIOGRAPHY

Botanical Society of America. "Carnivorous Plants/Insectivorous Plants." *Carnivorous Plant Pages.* N.d. http://www.botany.org/carnivorous%5Fplants/ (October 11, 2006).

D'Amato, Peter. *The Savage Garden.* Berkeley, CA: Ten Speed Press, 1998.

Edwards, Paul. *Victorian Carnivorous Plant Society, Inc.* September 2, 2006. http://www.vcps.au.com/ (October 11, 2006).

Ellison, Aaron. "Nitrogen Availability Alters the Expression of Carnivory in the Northern Pitcher Plant, *Sarracenia Purpurea.*" *PNAS.* April 2, 2002. http://www.pnas.org/cgi/content/abstract/99/7/4409 (October 11, 2006).

Flora of North America Association. *Introduction to North American Carnivorous Plants Fact Sheet.* 2004. http://hua.huh.harvard.edu/FNA/Outreach/FNA_fsintro_carnivory.shtml (October 11, 2006).

ICPS. *International Carnivorous Plant Society.* N.d. http://www.carnivorousplants.org/ (October 11, 2006).

Miller, Matt. *Carnivorous Plants Online.* March 2004. http://home.paonline.com/mrmiller/ (October 11, 2006).

"Notable Natives." *Center for Plant Conservation.* N.d. http://www.centerforplantconservation.org/peril/peril11.html (October 11, 2006).

Rice, Barry. *Barry Rice's Carnivorous Plants Page.* September 2006. http://www.sarracenia.com/ (October 11, 2006).

Rice, Barry. "The Carnivorous Plant FAQ, v. 10.0: Courtesy of The International Carnivorous Plant Society." *Barry Rice's Carnivorous Plants Page.* September 2006. http://www.sarracenia.com/faq.html (October 11, 2006).

Rice, Barry. *Growing Carnivorous Plants.* Portland, OR: Timber Press, 2006.

Schnell, Donald. *Carnivorous Plants of the United States and Canada.* Portland, OR: Timber Press, 2002.

Slack, Adrian. *Carnivorous Plants.* Cambridge, MA: MIT Press, 2000.

Walker, Rick. "Carnivorous Plant Database."*OmnisTerra.* August 25, 2006. http://www.omnisterra.com/bot/cp_home.cgi (October 11, 2006).

WEBSITES

Botanical Society of America Carnivorous Plant Pages
http://www.botany.org/carnivorous_plants
Visit this website to read interesting information and view amazing pictures of carnivorous plants.

Environmental Kids Club
http://www.epa.gov/kids
This page from the U.S. Environmental Protection Agency features links to useful sites on plants and animals, air and water, the environment, and more.

Science News for Kids
http://www.sciencenewsforkids.org
At this site, you can read articles on plants, weather, Earth, and many other science-related topics.

FURTHER READING

Goodman, Susan E. *Seeds, Stems, and Stamens: The Ways Plants Fit into Their World.* Minneapolis: Millbrook Press, 2001.

Halfmann, Janet. *Plant Tricksters.* New York: Franklin Watts, 2003.

Halpern, Monica. *Venus Flytraps, Bladderworts, and Other Wild and Amazing Plants.* Washington, DC: National Geographic, 2006.

Hershey, David R. *Plant Biology Science Projects.* New York: John Wiley and Sons, 1995.

Souza, D. M. *Meat-Eating Plants.* New York: Franklin Watts, 2002.

INDEX

ABOUT THE AUTHOR

Rebecca L. Johnson is the author of dozens of books for children and young adults, including the award-winning Biomes of North America series. Johnson grew up on the Great Plains, where she spent as much time as possible outdoors, exploring the prairie landscape. She saw her first Venus flytrap at a botanic garden while still in grade school.

PHOTO ACKNOWLEDGMENTS

The images in this book are used with the permission of: © Jeno Kapitany/Collectors Corner, all backgrounds on pp. 1, 5, 8, 10, 13, 14, 15, 16, 19, 28, 32, 37, 38, 41, 42, 44, 45, 46, 47, 48; © Lonely Planet Images/Getty Images, p. 2–3; © Altrendo/Getty Images, p. 4; © Jerome Wexler/Visuals Unlimited, pp. 5 (inset), 18, 32; © Fritz Polking/Visuals Unlimited, p. 6; © Barry Rice/Visuals Unlimited, pp. 7, 10 (inset), 12, 15 (top), 19 (inset), 20, 26, 33, 37 (inset), 39, 40; © Dwight R. Kuhn, pp. 8, 24, 25, 27, 34 (both); © David Sieren/Visuals Unlimited, pp. 9, 13 (right), 14 (inset); © Laura Westlund/Independent Picture Service, p. 11; © T. Vandersar/SuperStock, p. 13 (left); © Claude Nuridsany & Marie Perennou/Photo Researchers, Inc., pp. 15 (bottom), 29; © National Geographic/Getty Images, p. 16; © Claus Meyer/Minden Pictures, p. 17 (bottom); © Mark Moffett/Minden Pictures, pp. 21, 22; © age fotostock/ SuperStock, p. 23; © Ernest Manewal/SuperStock, p. 28 (inset); © Bill Beatty/Visuals Unlimited, p. 30; © Taxi/Getty Images, p. 31; © Sir Ghillean Prance/Visuals Unlimited, p. 35; © Perennou Nuridsany/Photo Researchers, Inc., p. 36; © Frans Lanting/Minden Pictures, p. 38; © Getty Images, p. 41 (inset); © Lynda Richardson/CORBIS, pp. 42, 43.

Front cover: © Neil Miller; Papilio/CORBIS

Back cover: © Jeno Kapitany/Collectors Corner